The History of Nigeria

Copyright © 2023 by Adeoye Adekunle and Einar Felix Hansen. All rights reserved.

This book was created with the help of Artificial Intelligence and is protected by copyright law. No part of this book may be reproduced or transmitted in any form or by any means, electronic or mechanical, including photocopying, recording, or by any information storage and retrieval system without the written permission of the author, except for brief quotations in a review.

The information and opinions expressed in this book are for entertainment purposes only and are not intended to provide any form of professional or expert advice. The author and publisher of this book shall not be liable for any direct, indirect, consequential, or incidental damages arising out of the use of, or inability to use, the information and opinions contained in this book.

While every effort has been made to ensure the accuracy and completeness of the information presented in this book, the author and publisher assume no responsibility for errors or omissions, or for damages resulting from the use of the information contained herein.

The Precolonial Era: Early Societies and Kingdoms 6

The Arrival of Europeans: Colonialism and the Slave Trade 9

Resistance and Rebellion: Anti-Colonial Movements 11

Independence and Nation Building: The First Republic 14

Military Rule and Dictatorship: The Second Republic 16

Economic Development and Petroleum Wealth 18

Regionalism and Ethnic Politics: The Third Republic 20

Military Coup and the Rise of General Sani Abacha 22

Transition to Democracy: The Fourth Republic 24

Nigeria's Political System: Federalism, State, and Local Governance 27

Religion and Culture in Nigeria 29

Nigeria's Population: Ethnic Diversity and Demographic Trends 32

The Role of Women in Nigerian Society 35

The Nigerian Diaspora: History and Impact 37

Education in Nigeria: Challenges and Opportunities 39

Healthcare in Nigeria: Access and Quality Issues 42

The Nigerian Economy: Growth, Inequality, and Poverty 45

Agriculture and Food Security in Nigeria 47

Oil and Gas in Nigeria: Resource Curse or Blessing? 50

Environmental Challenges in Nigeria: Climate Change and Pollution 53

Infrastructure and Transportation: Road, Rail, and Air Travel 55

Media and Communication in Nigeria: Free Speech and Censorship 57

The Arts in Nigeria: Literature, Music, and Film 59

Sports in Nigeria: Football, Athletics, and Other Popular Activities 61

Nigeria's Future: Challenges and Prospects for the 21st Century 63

Conclusion 65

The Precolonial Era: Early Societies and Kingdoms

Nigeria's history dates back thousands of years before the arrival of European explorers and colonizers. The precolonial era of Nigeria's history is marked by the emergence of a diverse range of societies and kingdoms, each with its unique culture, economy, and political organization. In this chapter, we will delve into the early societies and kingdoms that existed in Nigeria before the arrival of Europeans.

Geographically, Nigeria occupies a significant portion of West Africa, covering a land area of approximately 923,769 square kilometers. The earliest human settlements in Nigeria are believed to have originated around 10,000 BCE, in the Jos Plateau region of central Nigeria. These early settlers were hunters and gatherers who relied on the natural resources of the region for survival.

Around 3000 BCE, the development of agriculture and animal husbandry transformed the way of life of these early settlers, leading to the emergence of settled communities and the development of local economies. Over time, these communities grew in size and complexity, leading to the emergence of organized societies and kingdoms.

One of the earliest known kingdoms in Nigeria was the Nok culture, which emerged around 1500 BCE in what is now central Nigeria. The Nok people were known for their advanced ironworking skills, and their artifacts, including terracotta sculptures, are still revered as masterpieces of African art.

Another significant precolonial kingdom was the Kanem-Borno empire, which emerged in the 9th century CE in the Lake Chad region of northeastern Nigeria. The Kanem-Borno empire was renowned for its military prowess and its thriving trade networks, which extended to North Africa and the Middle East. The empire was also known for its cultural achievements, including the development of a written script called the Kanuri alphabet.

In the western part of Nigeria, the Yoruba people developed a sophisticated system of governance and social organization. The Yoruba kingdoms, including the Oyo Empire and the Ife kingdom, were known for their artistic and architectural achievements, including the creation of intricate terracotta and bronze sculptures and the construction of impressive buildings such as the Oyo palace.

In the southeast of Nigeria, the Igbo people developed a decentralized system of government that emphasized individual autonomy and community decision-making. The Igbo were known for their trading skills and their sophisticated crafts, including pottery and weaving.

Throughout Nigeria's precolonial era, there was a great deal of cultural exchange and interaction between different societies and kingdoms. Trade networks, marriage alliances, and religious beliefs all contributed to the sharing of ideas and practices between different groups.

Despite this cultural exchange, there were also periods of conflict and warfare between different societies and kingdoms. The trans-Saharan slave trade, which flourished from the 8th to the 16th century, also had a significant impact on the social and political organization of Nigeria's precolonial societies.

In conclusion, Nigeria's precolonial era was a time of great diversity and complexity, marked by the emergence of numerous societies and kingdoms with their unique culture, economy, and political organization. The legacy of these early societies and kingdoms can still be seen in Nigeria's rich cultural heritage today.

The Arrival of Europeans: Colonialism and the Slave Trade

The arrival of Europeans in Nigeria in the 15th century marked a significant turning point in the country's history. The Portuguese were the first to arrive, followed by the British, Dutch, and French. The arrival of these European powers had a profound impact on the social, economic, and political landscape of Nigeria, leading to the transatlantic slave trade, colonization, and the exploitation of Nigeria's natural resources.

One of the primary drivers of European interest in Nigeria was the desire for slave labor. Europeans established trading posts along the coast of Nigeria, where they exchanged goods such as textiles, firearms, and alcohol for enslaved people who were then transported to the Americas to work on plantations. The transatlantic slave trade had a devastating impact on Nigeria's population, with an estimated 2 million people taken from the region and sold into slavery between the 15th and 19th centuries.

As the slave trade declined in the 19th century, European powers turned their attention to colonizing Nigeria. In 1861, Lagos became a British colony, and over the next few decades, the British extended their control over the rest of Nigeria. The French also established colonies in the north of Nigeria, while the Germans and Portuguese had smaller colonies in the southeast and southwest, respectively.

Colonialism had a profound impact on Nigeria's social, economic, and political development. European powers established colonial administrations, which imposed their own legal systems and bureaucracy on Nigeria. The British, in particular, were interested in exploiting Nigeria's natural resources, such as palm oil and rubber, which led to the forced labor of Nigerians in mining and plantation work.

The colonial period also saw the introduction of Christianity and Western education to Nigeria, which had a significant impact on the country's cultural and intellectual life. Missionaries established schools and hospitals, which helped to spread literacy and improve healthcare, but also led to the erosion of traditional cultural practices.

Resistance to colonial rule was a constant theme throughout Nigeria's colonial period. Nigerians who opposed colonialism formed political movements and nationalist organizations, such as the National Council of Nigeria and the Cameroons (NCNC) and the Nigerian Youth Movement (NYM). These movements were often met with violence and repression from colonial authorities, with leaders such as Nnamdi Azikiwe and Obafemi Awolowo being arrested and imprisoned for their activism.

In conclusion, the arrival of Europeans in Nigeria marked the beginning of a new era in the country's history, one marked by the transatlantic slave trade, colonization, and the exploitation of Nigeria's natural resources. The legacy of colonialism can still be seen in Nigeria today, with many of the country's social, economic, and political structures reflecting the influence of European powers.

Resistance and Rebellion: Anti-Colonial Movements

The arrival of European powers in Nigeria in the 15th century marked the beginning of centuries of exploitation, violence, and oppression. The transatlantic slave trade and colonialism had a profound impact on the country, leading to the exploitation of Nigeria's natural resources, the erosion of traditional cultures and practices, and the subjugation of its people. However, Nigeria was not passive in the face of colonialism. Throughout the colonial period, resistance and rebellion were a constant theme in Nigerian history, as Nigerians fought for their freedom, dignity, and rights.

One of the earliest forms of resistance to colonialism was the emergence of secret societies, such as the Ekpe and Ogboni, which organized resistance against European powers. These societies were often seen as a threat to colonial rule and were subjected to violent repression by colonial authorities.

The nationalist movement in Nigeria emerged in the early 20th century, with the formation of organizations such as the National Council of Nigeria and the Cameroons (NCNC) and the Nigerian Youth Movement (NYM). These organizations sought to mobilize Nigerians against colonialism and fight for independence. The nationalists organized protests, strikes, and boycotts, which challenged colonial authority and put pressure on the British government to recognize Nigeria's demand for self-rule.

One of the most significant anti-colonial movements in Nigeria was the Egba Women's War of 1929. This rebellion was sparked by the imposition of taxes on market women by colonial authorities. Thousands of women from the Egba ethnic group mobilized and marched to protest against the taxes, which they saw as an attempt to erode their economic independence and undermine their authority. The women's war was a significant moment in Nigerian history, as it demonstrated the power of women in resisting colonialism.

The struggle for independence in Nigeria culminated in the formation of the Nigerian National Democratic Party (NNDP) in 1923, which was later renamed the National Party of Nigeria (NPN) in 1979. The NPN was a major force in the struggle for independence, and in 1960, Nigeria gained its independence from Britain. However, independence did not mean the end of the struggle for Nigerians. The new Nigerian government was often corrupt and repressive, leading to renewed resistance and rebellion.

One of the most significant anti-colonial movements in post-independence Nigeria was the Biafran War of 1967-1970. The Biafran War was fought between the Nigerian government and the secessionist state of Biafra, which had declared independence from Nigeria. The war was marked by violence, starvation, and atrocities committed by both sides. The Biafran War was a significant moment in Nigerian history, as it highlighted the challenges of national unity and the tensions between different ethnic groups in Nigeria.

In conclusion, resistance and rebellion were a constant theme in Nigerian history, as Nigerians fought against colonialism, oppression, and exploitation. The legacy of these struggles can still be seen in Nigeria today, with many Nigerians continuing to fight for their rights, dignity, and freedom.

Independence and Nation Building: The First Republic

Nigeria gained its independence from British colonial rule on October 1, 1960, marking the beginning of a new era in Nigerian history. The First Republic, which lasted from 1960 to 1966, was a period of optimism and hope, as Nigerians sought to build a democratic and prosperous nation.

One of the major challenges facing Nigeria after independence was the need to build a new political system. The country adopted a federal system of government, which provided for a central government and several regional governments. The federal system was intended to balance power between the central government and the regions, which were based on Nigeria's major ethnic groups.

The first elections in Nigeria after independence were held in 1964, and the Nigerian National Democratic Party (NNDP) won a majority of seats in the federal parliament. Sir Abubakar Tafawa Balewa, leader of the NNDP, became Nigeria's first Prime Minister.

The First Republic was marked by significant economic growth, driven by Nigeria's rich natural resources, including oil. Nigeria became a member of the Organization of Petroleum Exporting Countries (OPEC) in 1971, which gave the country a significant voice in global oil politics.

Despite this economic growth, there were significant challenges facing Nigeria during the First Republic. One of the major challenges was the issue of regionalism and ethnic tensions. Nigeria's regions were based on ethnic groups, and there was often competition and conflict between different regions. The federal system of government was intended to address these tensions, but it often led to power struggles between the central government and the regions.

The First Republic was also marked by political instability, with several coups and attempted coups taking place. The first military coup in Nigeria occurred in January 1966, when a group of army officers led by Major Chukwuma Kaduna Nzeogwu overthrew the government of Sir Abubakar Tafawa Balewa. This coup was followed by several others, including one in July 1966, which led to the eventual collapse of the First Republic.

In conclusion, the First Republic was a significant period in Nigerian history, as the country gained its independence from colonial rule and sought to build a democratic and prosperous nation. Despite significant economic growth, the First Republic was marked by challenges, including regionalism and ethnic tensions, and political instability. The legacy of the First Republic can still be seen in Nigeria today, as the country continues to grapple with these challenges and strives to build a better future for all Nigerians.

Military Rule and Dictatorship: The Second Republic

The Second Republic in Nigeria was a period of military rule and dictatorship that lasted from 1979 to 1983. This period was marked by political repression, corruption, and human rights abuses, which had a significant impact on the country's development and its people.

The Second Republic began in 1979, with the election of Shehu Shagari as Nigeria's second civilian president. However, Shagari's government was soon beset by economic problems, including inflation and a decline in oil revenues. These economic problems led to widespread discontent among the Nigerian people, which was further exacerbated by allegations of corruption and political repression.

In 1983, General Muhammadu Buhari staged a coup and overthrew the government of Shehu Shagari. Buhari's government was marked by authoritarianism and a crackdown on political opposition. The government introduced strict laws on press freedom and banned political parties, leading to a significant decline in civil liberties.

Buhari's government was also marked by its focus on the fight against corruption. The government introduced measures to combat corruption, including the establishment of a Special Military Tribunal to try corrupt officials. However, these measures were often criticized for their lack of transparency and for targeting political opponents.

Buhari's government was short-lived, and in 1985, he was overthrown in a coup led by General Ibrahim Babangida. Babangida's government was marked by a more liberal approach to politics, with the reintroduction of political parties and a greater emphasis on economic development.

However, Babangida's government was also marked by corruption and political repression. The government was accused of rigging elections, and political opposition was often met with violence and intimidation. Babangida's government also faced challenges from ethnic and religious tensions, particularly in the northern and southern regions of the country.

In 1993, Babangida annulled the presidential elections, which were widely believed to have been won by the opposition candidate Moshood Abiola. This led to widespread protests and unrest, which were met with violence by the government.

In conclusion, the Second Republic in Nigeria was marked by military rule and dictatorship, with significant challenges to civil liberties and political opposition. The legacy of this period can still be seen in Nigeria today, with many Nigerians continuing to fight for democracy and human rights.

Economic Development and Petroleum Wealth

Nigeria's economy has undergone significant changes since independence. The discovery of oil in the late 1950s and early 1960s transformed Nigeria's economy and had a profound impact on the country's development.

Nigeria is now the largest producer of oil in Africa, and the petroleum sector accounts for over 80% of Nigeria's total export revenue. However, the reliance on oil exports has also had significant economic and social consequences.

One of the major impacts of petroleum wealth on Nigeria's economy has been the neglect of other sectors. Agriculture, which was once a significant contributor to Nigeria's economy, has been largely neglected, leading to a decline in food production and a dependence on imports. This has led to significant food insecurity in Nigeria, with millions of Nigerians facing chronic hunger and malnutrition.

The reliance on oil exports has also led to the deindustrialization of Nigeria's economy. The country has become dependent on imported goods, leading to a decline in local manufacturing and industry. This has had significant consequences for Nigeria's job market, with high levels of unemployment and underemployment.

Despite these challenges, the petroleum sector has also had significant benefits for Nigeria's economy. The revenue from oil exports has been used to fund major infrastructure projects, including roads, bridges, and airports. The petroleum sector has also created jobs in related industries, such as shipping, logistics, and services.

The Nigerian government has attempted to diversify the country's economy and reduce its reliance on oil exports. The government has introduced policies to encourage investment in agriculture, manufacturing, and industry. However, these efforts have often been undermined by corruption, political instability, and insecurity.

In recent years, Nigeria has faced significant economic challenges, including the decline in oil prices, the devaluation of the national currency, and the impact of the COVID-19 pandemic. These challenges have highlighted the need for Nigeria to diversify its economy and invest in other sectors, such as renewable energy, technology, and services.

In conclusion, Nigeria's economy has been transformed by the discovery of oil and the growth of the petroleum sector. While this has had significant benefits for Nigeria's development, it has also led to challenges, including the neglect of other sectors and the dependence on oil exports. The legacy of petroleum wealth can still be seen in Nigeria today, as the country continues to grapple with the need for economic diversification and the challenges of building a more prosperous and sustainable economy.

Regionalism and Ethnic Politics: The Third Republic

The Third Republic in Nigeria, which lasted from 1993 to 1999, was marked by regionalism and ethnic politics. The period was characterized by political instability, economic challenges, and significant social unrest.

The Third Republic began with the presidential election of 1993, which was widely regarded as the freest and fairest election in Nigeria's history. The election was won by Moshood Abiola, a businessman and philanthropist who had widespread support across the country.

However, the military government annulled the election, leading to widespread protests and unrest. The annulment of the election highlighted the deep divisions in Nigerian society, particularly along regional and ethnic lines.

The political crisis was further exacerbated by the death of General Sani Abacha, who had taken power in a military coup in 1993. Abacha's death led to the appointment of General Abdulsalami Abubakar as the new head of state, who initiated a transition to civilian rule.

The Third Republic was characterized by the rise of regional and ethnic politics. Political parties were often organized along regional and ethnic lines, with little emphasis on national unity or development. The country was also beset by social unrest, including communal violence, ethnic clashes, and religious conflicts.

One of the major challenges facing the Third Republic was the issue of corruption. Corruption was widespread throughout Nigerian society, from the highest levels of government to everyday transactions. Corruption had significant economic consequences, undermining development and leading to a decline in public trust and social cohesion.

Despite these challenges, the Third Republic also saw some significant achievements. The government introduced economic reforms, including the deregulation of the economy and the privatization of state-owned enterprises. These reforms led to significant economic growth, with Nigeria's GDP growing by an average of 7% per year during the Third Republic.

The Third Republic was also marked by the struggle for democracy and human rights. Civil society organizations and human rights activists played a significant role in challenging authoritarianism and promoting political reform. The struggle for democracy culminated in the adoption of a new constitution in 1999, which paved the way for the Fourth Republic.

In conclusion, the Third Republic in Nigeria was marked by regionalism and ethnic politics, with significant challenges to national unity and development. The legacy of this period can still be seen in Nigeria today, with the country continuing to grapple with the challenges of building a more inclusive and equitable society. The struggle for democracy and human rights that characterized the Third Republic remains a significant part of Nigeria's political and social landscape.

Military Coup and the Rise of General Sani Abacha

The period between the late 1980s and mid-1990s in Nigeria was marked by political instability, economic challenges, and social unrest. The country was beset by corruption, ethnic tensions, and authoritarianism, leading to a series of military coups and a decline in civil liberties.

One of the major events during this period was the rise of General Sani Abacha, who took power in a military coup in November 1993. Abacha's regime was marked by authoritarianism, corruption, and human rights abuses, and had a significant impact on Nigeria's development and its people.

Abacha was born in Kano state in northern Nigeria in 1943. He joined the Nigerian army in 1963 and rose through the ranks, becoming a major general in 1985. Abacha was appointed as Minister of Defence in 1990 by General Ibrahim Babangida, who was then the head of state.

Abacha's rise to power came after the annulment of the presidential election of 1993, which had been widely regarded as free and fair. The annulment of the election sparked widespread protests and unrest, and Abacha saw an opportunity to seize power.

Abacha's regime was characterized by authoritarianism and repression. The government introduced strict laws on press freedom and political opposition, leading to a decline in civil liberties. The government was also accused of human rights abuses, including extrajudicial killings, torture, and detention without trial.

Corruption was widespread throughout Abacha's government, with billions of dollars siphoned off from the country's oil revenues. Abacha's family and associates became extremely wealthy, while ordinary Nigerians faced significant economic challenges.

Abacha's government was also marked by its focus on Nigeria's ethnic and regional tensions. The government was accused of stoking ethnic tensions and sponsoring communal violence, particularly in the northern regions of the country.

The international community also played a significant role in challenging Abacha's regime. The government was subject to economic sanctions and diplomatic pressure from Western countries, who were concerned about human rights abuses and corruption in Nigeria.

Abacha died suddenly in June 1998, leading to the eventual transition to civilian rule in Nigeria. The legacy of Abacha's regime can still be seen in Nigeria today, with the country continuing to grapple with the challenges of corruption, authoritarianism, and ethnic tensions.

In conclusion, the rise of General Sani Abacha and his regime had a significant impact on Nigerian history. Abacha's government was marked by authoritarianism, corruption, and human rights abuses, and had a profound impact on Nigeria's development and its people. The legacy of Abacha's regime can still be seen in Nigeria today, as the country continues to grapple with the challenges of building a more democratic and inclusive society.

Transition to Democracy: The Fourth Republic

The Fourth Republic in Nigeria began in 1999, following the adoption of a new constitution and the election of Olusegun Obasanjo as Nigeria's first civilian president in over a decade. The Fourth Republic marked a significant shift in Nigerian politics, as the country sought to rebuild its democracy and promote human rights and development.

The transition to democracy was a significant moment in Nigerian history. It followed years of military rule and dictatorship, marked by corruption, repression, and human rights abuses. The adoption of a new constitution and the holding of free and fair elections were seen as important steps in rebuilding Nigeria's political system.

The Fourth Republic was characterized by a focus on democracy, human rights, and economic development. The government introduced policies aimed at promoting civil liberties, such as freedom of speech and the press, and strengthening the rule of law. The government also introduced measures to promote economic growth and development, including reforms in the energy, telecommunications, and agriculture sectors.

One of the major challenges facing the Fourth Republic was the issue of corruption. Corruption had been endemic in Nigerian society for decades, and it had a significant impact on the country's development and its people. The government introduced measures aimed at combating corruption, including the establishment of an anti-corruption agency, the Economic and Financial Crimes Commission (EFCC).

The Fourth Republic was also marked by the struggle for human rights and social justice. Civil society organizations, human rights activists, and the media played a significant role in promoting human rights and challenging abuses by the government and other actors. The government was often criticized for its handling of human rights issues, including police brutality, extrajudicial killings, and violations of the rights of minorities and marginalized groups.

The Fourth Republic also saw significant progress in Nigerian politics. The country held several successful presidential and parliamentary elections, which were widely regarded as free and fair. The Fourth Republic also saw the emergence of a more diverse political landscape, with the rise of opposition parties and independent candidates.

Despite these achievements, the Fourth Republic was also marked by significant challenges. The country continued to grapple with corruption, economic inequality, and insecurity. The government also faced significant challenges in addressing the needs and concerns of marginalized groups, such as women, youth, and the rural poor.

In conclusion, the Fourth Republic in Nigeria marked a significant shift in the country's political and social landscape. The transition to democracy and the promotion of human rights and development were important steps in rebuilding Nigeria's political system. However, the Fourth Republic was also marked by challenges, including corruption, inequality, and insecurity. The legacy of the Fourth Republic can still be seen in Nigeria today, as the country continues to grapple with these challenges and work towards building a more inclusive and equitable society.

Nigeria's Political System: Federalism, State, and Local Governance

Nigeria's political system is based on a federal structure, with power divided between the federal government, the 36 states, and the local government areas. This system was introduced in 1963 and has undergone several changes over the years, including the adoption of a new constitution in 1999.

The federal government is responsible for matters of national importance, such as defense, foreign policy, and the economy. The federal government is led by the president, who is elected every four years, and is responsible for appointing ministers and other key officials.

The 36 states in Nigeria have their own governments, which are responsible for matters of state importance, such as education, health care, and infrastructure. The states are led by governors, who are elected every four years, and are responsible for appointing commissioners and other key officials.

Local government areas are responsible for the provision of basic services, such as water, sanitation, and primary education. There are 774 local government areas in Nigeria, each of which is led by a chairman and a council.

The federal system in Nigeria has been a source of both strength and weakness. On the one hand, it has allowed for greater regional autonomy and the sharing of power between the federal government and the states. This has enabled the states to tailor policies to local needs and respond to local challenges.

On the other hand, the federal system has also led to challenges, including corruption, inefficiency, and a lack of accountability. The sharing of power between the federal government and the states has sometimes led to confusion and conflict over jurisdiction and responsibilities.

In recent years, there have been calls for a restructuring of Nigeria's federal system, with some advocating for greater devolution of power to the states and local government areas. This debate has centered on issues such as resource control, revenue allocation, and the distribution of political power.

Despite these challenges, Nigeria's political system has undergone significant changes over the years, reflecting the country's complex political, social, and economic landscape. The adoption of a new constitution in 1999 and the transition to civilian rule marked important steps in Nigeria's journey towards democracy and good governance.

In conclusion, Nigeria's political system is based on a federal structure, with power divided between the federal government, the 36 states, and the local government areas. The federal system has enabled greater regional autonomy and tailored policies to local needs, but has also led to challenges such as corruption and inefficiency. The ongoing debate over the restructuring of Nigeria's federal system reflects the country's complex political and social landscape and highlights the need for ongoing reforms and good governance.

Religion and Culture in Nigeria

Nigeria is a country with a diverse mix of religions and cultures, reflecting its complex history and geography. The country is home to over 250 ethnic groups, each with their own unique cultures and traditions. Religion is also a significant part of Nigerian society, with Christianity, Islam, and traditional African religions being the most widely practiced.

Christianity was introduced to Nigeria by European missionaries in the 19th century and has since become one of the largest religions in the country. The majority of Christians in Nigeria are Roman Catholic or Protestant, with a significant number of Pentecostals and evangelicals. Christianity has had a significant impact on Nigerian culture, influencing music, art, and literature.

Islam was also introduced to Nigeria by Arab traders and has become one of the largest religions in the country. The majority of Muslims in Nigeria are Sunni, with a significant number of Shia Muslims. Islam has also had a significant impact on Nigerian culture, influencing art, architecture, and literature.

Traditional African religions are also practiced in Nigeria, particularly in rural areas. These religions are often based on the worship of ancestors and nature spirits and are characterized by a strong emphasis on community and social ties. Traditional African religions have had a significant impact on Nigerian culture, influencing music, dance, and art.

Nigeria's diverse mix of religions and cultures has led to a rich and vibrant cultural heritage. Nigerian music, literature, and art are known for their diversity and creativity, drawing on a range of influences from across the country and beyond. Nigerian music is particularly popular across Africa, with Nigerian musicians such as Fela Kuti and Wizkid achieving international acclaim.

Despite the richness and diversity of Nigerian culture, there are also challenges facing cultural preservation and development. The rapid pace of urbanization and globalization has led to the decline of traditional cultural practices and the homogenization of cultural expressions. There is also a need for greater investment in cultural institutions, such as museums and cultural centers, to promote cultural awareness and preservation.

Religion has also played a significant role in Nigerian society and politics. Religious organizations and leaders have often been influential in shaping public opinion and advocating for social and political change. However, religion has also been a source of conflict and division, particularly between Christians and Muslims.

In recent years, there have been efforts to promote interfaith dialogue and understanding, as well as greater cultural awareness and preservation. These efforts have been supported by government policies and initiatives, as well as by civil society organizations and cultural institutions.

In conclusion, Nigeria's diverse mix of religions and cultures has led to a rich and vibrant cultural heritage, with music, literature, and art drawing on a range of influences. However, there are also challenges facing cultural preservation and development, as well as the need for greater interfaith dialogue and understanding. The ongoing promotion of cultural awareness and preservation is essential for ensuring the continued vibrancy and diversity of Nigeria's cultural heritage.

Nigeria's Population: Ethnic Diversity and Demographic Trends

Nigeria is the most populous country in Africa, with a population of over 200 million people. The country is home to over 250 ethnic groups, each with their own unique languages, cultures, and traditions. Nigeria's population is also characterized by significant demographic trends, including population growth, urbanization, and youth bulges.

The three largest ethnic groups in Nigeria are the Hausa-Fulani in the north, the Yoruba in the southwest, and the Igbo in the southeast. However, there are also significant populations of other ethnic groups, including the Edo, Ijaw, Kanuri, Tiv, and Nupe, among others. Ethnic diversity in Nigeria has led to a rich and diverse cultural heritage, with each group contributing to the country's music, art, and literature.

Population growth in Nigeria has been a significant trend over the years, with the country's population doubling in size over the last few decades. This growth has been driven by high fertility rates, a decline in mortality rates, and increased life expectancy. The rapid population growth has led to significant challenges, including pressure on social services, infrastructure, and natural resources.

Urbanization is another significant demographic trend in Nigeria, with a significant percentage of the population living in urban areas. The growth of cities has led to significant changes in Nigerian society and culture, with new opportunities and challenges for social and economic development. Urbanization has also contributed to the decline of traditional cultural practices and the rise of new cultural expressions. Nigeria's population is also characterized by a significant youth bulge, with over half of the population under the age of 25. This presents both opportunities and challenges, with the potential for a large, educated workforce and innovative entrepreneurship, but also the risk of unemployment, social unrest, and political instability.

Demographic trends in Nigeria have significant implications for the country's development and future prospects. Addressing challenges such as population growth, urbanization, and youth bulges will require comprehensive policies and programs, as well as investment in social services and infrastructure. In recent years, there have been efforts to promote sustainable population growth, including programs aimed at promoting family planning and reproductive health. The government has also prioritized investment in infrastructure and social services, such as education and health care, to support the growing population.

In conclusion, Nigeria's population is characterized by ethnic diversity, significant demographic trends, and challenges. The country's rich and diverse cultural heritage is a reflection of its ethnic diversity, with each group contributing to the country's music, art, and literature. Demographic trends such as population growth, urbanization, and youth bulges present significant challenges for the country's development, but also opportunities for social and economic progress. Addressing these challenges will require comprehensive policies and programs, as well as investment in social services and infrastructure.

The Role of Women in Nigerian Society

The role of women in Nigerian society has undergone significant changes over the years, reflecting the country's complex political, social, and economic landscape. Women have played a significant role in Nigeria's development and progress, but also face significant challenges and obstacles.

Nigeria has a rich history of powerful and influential women, including Queen Amina of Zazzau in the 16th century and Funmilayo Ransome-Kuti, a prominent women's rights activist in the 20th century. Women have also played a significant role in Nigerian politics, with women serving as governors, ministers, and members of parliament.

Despite these achievements, women in Nigeria still face significant challenges and obstacles. Women continue to face discrimination and marginalization in various areas, including education, health care, and employment. Violence against women, including domestic violence and rape, remains a significant issue in Nigerian society.

One of the major challenges facing women in Nigeria is access to education. Although there has been progress in recent years, girls still face significant barriers to education, including poverty, cultural attitudes, and early marriage. Addressing these challenges will require comprehensive policies and programs, as well as investment in education and infrastructure.

Another significant challenge facing women in Nigeria is access to health care. Women have a higher risk of maternal mortality, as well as other health issues such as HIV/AIDS, malaria, and malnutrition. Improving access to health care, particularly in rural areas, is essential for promoting women's health and well-being.

Women in Nigeria also face significant challenges in the workforce, with limited opportunities for women in leadership positions and significant pay disparities. Addressing these challenges will require comprehensive policies and programs, as well as investment in infrastructure and economic development.

In recent years, there have been efforts to promote gender equality and women's empowerment in Nigeria. The government has introduced policies aimed at promoting women's rights and addressing issues such as violence against women and discrimination. Civil society organizations and women's groups have also played a significant role in promoting women's rights and advocating for social and political change.

In conclusion, the role of women in Nigerian society is complex and multifaceted, reflecting both progress and challenges. Women have played a significant role in Nigeria's development and progress, but also face significant obstacles and discrimination. Addressing these challenges will require comprehensive policies and programs, as well as investment in education, health care, and economic development. The ongoing promotion of gender equality and women's empowerment is essential for building a more inclusive and equitable Nigerian society.

The Nigerian Diaspora: History and Impact

The Nigerian diaspora is a significant and diverse community, comprising Nigerians who have migrated to other countries for various reasons, including education, employment, and family reunification. The Nigerian diaspora is estimated to be around 17 million people, making it one of the largest in Africa.

The history of Nigerian migration dates back to the colonial era, when many Nigerians traveled to Europe and North America for education and employment opportunities. In the 1960s and 1970s, political instability and economic hardship led to significant migration to other African countries, particularly to Ghana and the Ivory Coast.

In recent years, there has been a significant increase in Nigerian migration to other countries, particularly to Europe and North America. The reasons for migration vary, but include a search for better economic opportunities, political instability, and conflict.

The Nigerian diaspora has had a significant impact on both Nigerian society and the countries in which they reside. In Nigeria, remittances from the diaspora have become a significant source of income, contributing to economic development and poverty reduction. The diaspora has also contributed to the development of various sectors, including education, health care, and technology.

In the countries in which they reside, Nigerians in the diaspora have made significant contributions to various sectors, including science, medicine, and the arts. Many Nigerians in the diaspora have achieved significant success in their fields, including Chimamanda Ngozi Adichie, a prominent author, and Wole Soyinka, a Nobel Prize-winning playwright.

The Nigerian diaspora has also played a significant role in promoting Nigerian culture and heritage, with various cultural festivals and events organized in countries around the world. These events showcase the diversity and richness of Nigerian culture, promoting cross-cultural exchange and understanding.

Despite these contributions, Nigerians in the diaspora also face significant challenges, including discrimination, xenophobia, and limited access to social services. The Nigerian government has introduced various initiatives aimed at supporting the diaspora, including the establishment of diaspora offices and the introduction of policies aimed at promoting investment and entrepreneurship.

In conclusion, the Nigerian diaspora is a significant and diverse community, comprising Nigerians who have migrated to other countries for various reasons. The diaspora has had a significant impact on both Nigerian society and the countries in which they reside, contributing to economic development, promoting cross-cultural exchange, and supporting various sectors, including education and health care. The ongoing promotion of diaspora engagement and support is essential for building stronger ties between Nigeria and the global community.

Education in Nigeria: Challenges and Opportunities

Education is a crucial component of Nigeria's development, providing the foundation for social and economic progress. However, education in Nigeria faces significant challenges, including limited access, inadequate funding, and poor quality. Addressing these challenges is essential for promoting a more inclusive and equitable society.

Access to education remains a significant challenge in Nigeria, particularly for girls and children from low-income families. According to UNESCO, Nigeria has one of the highest rates of out-of-school children in the world, with an estimated 10.5 million children not attending school. Factors such as poverty, cultural attitudes, and early marriage are significant barriers to education.

Inadequate funding is another significant challenge facing education in Nigeria. The country's education sector is severely underfunded, with many schools lacking basic infrastructure and resources. The low level of funding has also contributed to a significant decline in the quality of education, with many schools lacking qualified teachers and adequate teaching materials.

The poor quality of education is also a significant challenge, with many schools failing to provide a quality education that prepares students for the workforce. This has contributed to high levels of youth unemployment, particularly among graduates.

Despite these challenges, there are also opportunities for improving education in Nigeria. The government has introduced various initiatives aimed at promoting access to education, including the Universal Basic Education Program and the Girls Education Project. These programs aim to increase enrollment and retention rates, particularly for girls and children from low-income families.

The private sector has also played a significant role in promoting education in Nigeria, with many private schools and universities offering quality education to students. However, the high cost of private education remains a significant barrier for many families.

There is also a need for greater investment in teacher training and professional development, as well as in research and development. This will help to improve the quality of education and better prepare students for the workforce.

In recent years, there has been a growing recognition of the importance of technology in education, particularly in improving access and quality. The government has introduced various initiatives aimed at promoting the use of technology in education, including the introduction of e-learning platforms and the establishment of digital libraries.

In conclusion, education is a crucial component of Nigeria's development, providing the foundation for social and economic progress. However, education in Nigeria faces significant challenges, including limited access, inadequate funding, and poor quality. Addressing these challenges will require comprehensive policies and programs, as well as investment in teacher training, infrastructure, and technology. The ongoing promotion of education and lifelong learning is essential for building a more inclusive and equitable Nigerian society.

Healthcare in Nigeria: Access and Quality Issues

Access to quality healthcare is a crucial component of social and economic development, providing the foundation for a healthy and productive population. However, healthcare in Nigeria faces significant challenges, including limited access, inadequate funding, and poor quality. Addressing these challenges is essential for promoting a healthier and more productive society.

Access to healthcare remains a significant challenge in Nigeria, particularly in rural areas. Many Nigerians lack access to basic health services, including primary care and preventative measures. The country also faces significant shortages of healthcare workers, with a ratio of one doctor for every 5,000 people, significantly lower than the World Health Organization's recommended ratio of one doctor for every 600 people.

Inadequate funding is another significant challenge facing healthcare in Nigeria. The country's healthcare sector is severely underfunded, with many healthcare facilities lacking basic infrastructure and resources. The low level of funding has also contributed to a significant decline in the quality of healthcare, with many facilities lacking qualified healthcare workers and adequate medical equipment.

The poor quality of healthcare is also a significant challenge, with many facilities failing to provide quality care that meets international standards. This has contributed to high levels of morbidity and mortality, particularly among children and pregnant women.

Despite these challenges, there are also opportunities for improving healthcare in Nigeria. The government has introduced various initiatives aimed at promoting access to healthcare, including the National Health Insurance Scheme and the National Strategic Health Development Plan. These programs aim to increase access to healthcare services and improve the quality of care.

The private sector has also played a significant role in promoting healthcare in Nigeria, with many private hospitals and clinics offering quality healthcare services to patients. However, the high cost of private healthcare remains a significant barrier for many Nigerians.

There is also a need for greater investment in healthcare infrastructure and technology, as well as in healthcare worker training and professional development. This will help to improve the quality of healthcare and better prepare healthcare workers to provide quality care.

In recent years, there has been a growing recognition of the importance of technology in healthcare, particularly in improving access and quality. The government has introduced various initiatives aimed at promoting the use of technology in healthcare, including the introduction of electronic health records and telemedicine services.

In conclusion, healthcare is a crucial component of social and economic development, providing the foundation for a healthy and productive population. However, healthcare in Nigeria faces significant challenges, including limited access, inadequate funding, and poor quality. Addressing these challenges will require comprehensive policies and programs, as well as investment in healthcare infrastructure, technology, and healthcare worker training.

The ongoing promotion of healthcare and well-being is essential for building a healthier and more productive Nigerian society.

The Nigerian Economy: Growth, Inequality, and Poverty

The Nigerian economy is one of the largest in Africa, with a population of over 200 million and significant natural resources, including oil and gas. However, the economy faces significant challenges, including high levels of poverty and inequality, and limited diversification.

In recent years, Nigeria has experienced economic growth, with an average annual growth rate of around 6%. However, this growth has been uneven, with significant regional disparities and limited benefits for the poorest segments of the population. Poverty remains a significant challenge, with over 40% of Nigerians living below the poverty line.

Inequality is also a significant challenge in Nigeria, with a significant wealth gap between the rich and poor. This has contributed to social and political tensions, as well as limited social mobility for the poorest segments of the population.

Limited diversification is another significant challenge facing the Nigerian economy, with a heavy reliance on the oil and gas sector. This has made the economy vulnerable to fluctuations in global oil prices, contributing to economic instability and limited job opportunities outside of the oil and gas sector.

Addressing these challenges will require comprehensive policies and programs, as well as investment in infrastructure, education, and healthcare. The government has introduced various initiatives aimed at promoting economic diversification, including the Agricultural Transformation Agenda and the National Industrial Revolution Plan. These programs aim to promote growth and job creation outside of the oil and gas sector, particularly in agriculture and manufacturing.

The private sector has also played a significant role in promoting economic growth and job creation in Nigeria. However, limited access to finance and inadequate infrastructure remain significant barriers for many entrepreneurs.

There is also a need for greater investment in education and healthcare, particularly in addressing the significant regional disparities in access to these services. Improving access to education and healthcare is essential for promoting social and economic mobility and reducing poverty and inequality.

In conclusion, the Nigerian economy is one of the largest in Africa, with significant potential for growth and development. However, the economy faces significant challenges, including high levels of poverty and inequality, limited diversification, and regional disparities in access to social services. Addressing these challenges will require comprehensive policies and programs, as well as investment in infrastructure, education, and healthcare. The ongoing promotion of social and economic mobility is essential for building a more inclusive and equitable Nigerian society.

Agriculture and Food Security in Nigeria

Agriculture is a crucial sector of the Nigerian economy, providing employment opportunities for millions of people and contributing significantly to the country's GDP. However, the sector faces significant challenges, including limited access to credit, inadequate infrastructure, and low productivity. Addressing these challenges is essential for promoting food security and economic development in Nigeria.

Nigeria is endowed with significant natural resources and has vast agricultural potential. The country has a diverse climate, enabling the production of a wide range of crops, including cassava, yams, maize, and rice. Agriculture accounts for around 20% of Nigeria's GDP and provides employment opportunities for around 70% of the population.

However, the sector faces significant challenges, including limited access to credit, inadequate infrastructure, and low productivity. Limited access to credit is a significant barrier for many farmers, particularly smallholder farmers who lack collateral and credit history. Inadequate infrastructure, including poor road networks and limited access to electricity and water, also limits productivity and hinders the transportation of agricultural products to market.

The low productivity of the sector is another significant challenge, with many farmers using traditional farming methods and lacking access to modern technologies and best practices. This has contributed to low yields and limited income for many farmers.

Addressing these challenges will require comprehensive policies and programs, as well as investment in infrastructure and technology. The government has introduced various initiatives aimed at promoting agricultural development, including the Agricultural Transformation Agenda and the National Livestock Transformation Plan. These programs aim to promote productivity and increase access to credit and technology for smallholder farmers.

The private sector has also played a significant role in promoting agricultural development, particularly through investment in value chains and modern technologies. However, limited access to finance remains a significant barrier for many farmers and agribusinesses.

Improving food security is also a crucial component of agricultural development in Nigeria. Despite the country's agricultural potential, Nigeria faces significant food insecurity, with millions of people lacking access to nutritious food. This is due to a combination of factors, including limited access to credit and technology, inadequate infrastructure, and climate-related challenges.

Addressing food security will require a comprehensive approach, including policies and programs aimed at improving agricultural productivity, promoting income generation, and enhancing access to social services, including healthcare and education.

In conclusion, agriculture is a crucial sector of the Nigerian economy, providing employment opportunities and contributing significantly to the country's GDP. However, the sector faces significant challenges, including limited access to credit, inadequate infrastructure, and low productivity. Addressing these challenges is essential for promoting food security and economic development in Nigeria. The ongoing promotion of agricultural development and food security is essential for building a more resilient and sustainable Nigerian society.

Oil and Gas in Nigeria: Resource Curse or Blessing?

Nigeria is a major producer of oil and gas, with the sector accounting for a significant proportion of the country's GDP and exports. However, the sector also faces significant challenges, including environmental degradation, corruption, and social unrest. The question of whether oil and gas are a curse or a blessing for Nigeria is a complex one, with arguments on both sides.

On the one hand, oil and gas have provided significant revenue for the Nigerian government, enabling investment in social services and infrastructure. The sector has also provided employment opportunities for many Nigerians and contributed to the growth of other sectors of the economy, including banking and telecommunications.

However, the sector has also contributed to significant environmental degradation, particularly in the Niger Delta region. Oil spills and gas flaring have caused significant damage to the environment, including contamination of water sources and destruction of farmland. The environmental damage has also had a significant impact on the health and livelihoods of communities in the Niger Delta region.

Corruption is another significant challenge facing the oil and gas sector in Nigeria. The sector has been plagued by allegations of corruption and mismanagement, with many contracts and licenses awarded without due process. This has contributed to a lack of transparency and accountability, as well as significant revenue losses for the Nigerian government.

Social unrest is also a significant challenge facing the oil and gas sector in Nigeria, particularly in the Niger Delta region. The region has experienced significant social and political tensions, with many communities feeling marginalized and excluded from the benefits of oil and gas production. This has contributed to social unrest and political instability in the region.

Addressing these challenges will require comprehensive policies and programs, as well as investment in environmental management, transparency, and accountability. The government has introduced various initiatives aimed at promoting environmental sustainability and transparency in the sector, including the establishment of the Niger Delta Development Commission and the Extractive Industries Transparency Initiative.

The private sector has also played a significant role in promoting sustainable development in the oil and gas sector, particularly through investment in social and environmental programs. However, there is a need for greater collaboration between the public and private sectors to promote sustainable development and address the challenges facing the sector.

In conclusion, the oil and gas sector has provided significant revenue for the Nigerian government and contributed to economic growth and development. However, the sector also faces significant challenges, including environmental degradation, corruption, and social unrest. Addressing these challenges is essential for promoting sustainable development and ensuring that the sector benefits all Nigerians. The ongoing promotion of transparency, accountability, and environmental sustainability is essential for building a more equitable and sustainable Nigerian society.

Environmental Challenges in Nigeria: Climate Change and Pollution

Nigeria faces significant environmental challenges, including climate change and pollution. These challenges pose significant risks to the country's natural resources and human health, as well as to economic development and social stability. Addressing these challenges is essential for building a more sustainable and resilient Nigerian society.

Climate change is a significant challenge facing Nigeria, with rising temperatures and changes in rainfall patterns contributing to environmental degradation and food insecurity. The country's agricultural sector is particularly vulnerable to the impacts of climate change, with changes in rainfall patterns and rising temperatures affecting crop yields and food security.

Inadequate infrastructure is another significant challenge facing Nigeria's response to climate change. Limited access to electricity and clean water hinders the adoption of clean energy and water conservation technologies, contributing to increased greenhouse gas emissions and environmental degradation.

Pollution is also a significant challenge facing Nigeria, particularly in urban areas. Air pollution is a significant health risk, contributing to respiratory illnesses and other health issues. The country also faces significant water pollution, particularly in the Niger Delta region, where oil spills and gas flaring have caused significant environmental damage and health risks for local communities.

Addressing these challenges will require comprehensive policies and programs, as well as investment in infrastructure and technology. The government has introduced various initiatives aimed at promoting environmental sustainability, including the National Climate Change Policy and Response Strategy and the National Environmental Standards and Regulations Enforcement Agency.

The private sector has also played a significant role in promoting environmental sustainability, particularly through investment in clean energy and waste management technologies. However, there is a need for greater collaboration between the public and private sectors to promote sustainable development and address the challenges facing the environment.

Improving environmental sustainability is essential for promoting social and economic development, as well as for protecting human health and natural resources. The ongoing promotion of sustainable development and environmental sustainability is essential for building a more resilient and sustainable Nigerian society.

In conclusion, Nigeria faces significant environmental challenges, including climate change and pollution. Addressing these challenges will require comprehensive policies and programs, as well as investment in infrastructure and technology. The ongoing promotion of sustainable development and environmental sustainability is essential for building a more resilient and sustainable Nigerian society.

Infrastructure and Transportation: Road, Rail, and Air Travel

Infrastructure and transportation are crucial components of economic development and social mobility in Nigeria. However, the country faces significant challenges in these areas, including inadequate infrastructure and limited access to transportation. Addressing these challenges is essential for promoting economic growth and social development in Nigeria.

Road transportation is the most common mode of transportation in Nigeria, with the majority of the population relying on public transportation, including buses and motorcycles. However, the country's road infrastructure is inadequate, with limited road networks and poor road conditions. This has contributed to high rates of accidents and limited access to transportation for many Nigerians.

The government has introduced various initiatives aimed at improving road infrastructure, including the National Roads Fund and the Road Infrastructure Development and Refurbishment Investment Tax Credit Scheme. These programs aim to improve road conditions and increase access to transportation for all Nigerians.

Rail transportation is another mode of transportation in Nigeria, with the country's rail system covering around 3,500 kilometers. However, the country's rail system is limited, with inadequate infrastructure and limited passenger services. The government has introduced various initiatives aimed at promoting rail transportation, including the construction of new rail lines and the rehabilitation of existing ones.

Air transportation is also significant in Nigeria, particularly for international travel. The country has several international airports, including the Murtala Muhammed International Airport in Lagos and the Nnamdi Azikiwe International Airport in Abuja. However, the country's domestic air travel network is limited, with few airports and limited connectivity.

Improving infrastructure and transportation is essential for promoting economic growth and social development in Nigeria. The ongoing promotion of sustainable and efficient transportation networks is essential for building a more connected and inclusive Nigerian society.

In conclusion, infrastructure and transportation are crucial components of economic development and social mobility in Nigeria. However, the country faces significant challenges in these areas, including inadequate infrastructure and limited access to transportation. Addressing these challenges will require comprehensive policies and programs, as well as investment in infrastructure and technology. The ongoing promotion of sustainable and efficient transportation networks is essential for building a more connected and inclusive Nigerian society.

Media and Communication in Nigeria: Free Speech and Censorship

Media and communication play a crucial role in promoting democratic governance and facilitating the free flow of information in Nigeria. However, the country also faces significant challenges in these areas, including censorship and limited access to information. Addressing these challenges is essential for promoting free speech and democratic governance in Nigeria.

Nigeria has a vibrant media landscape, with a diverse range of print, broadcast, and online media outlets. The country's constitution guarantees freedom of speech and freedom of the press, and the media has played a crucial role in exposing corruption and holding the government accountable.

However, the media also faces significant challenges, including censorship and harassment. The government has used various tactics to censor the media, including the use of legal and regulatory frameworks, as well as physical intimidation and violence. Journalists and media outlets that are critical of the government or powerful interests are often targeted with legal action, harassment, and violence.

The government has also introduced various laws and regulations aimed at restricting freedom of speech and the press. These include the Cybercrimes Act, which criminalizes certain forms of online expression, and the National Broadcasting Commission Code, which imposes restrictions on broadcast content.

Despite these challenges, there are also opportunities for promoting free speech and democratic governance in Nigeria. The rise of social media and digital technologies has enabled greater access to information and facilitated the dissemination of alternative viewpoints. Civil society organizations and media advocacy groups have also played a significant role in promoting free speech and press freedom in Nigeria.

Addressing the challenges facing media and communication in Nigeria will require comprehensive policies and programs, as well as investment in technology and infrastructure. The government should work to promote freedom of speech and the press and create an enabling environment for the media to operate. This includes ensuring the independence of regulatory bodies and promoting transparency in the allocation of broadcast licenses and other resources.

In conclusion, media and communication play a crucial role in promoting democratic governance and facilitating the free flow of information in Nigeria. However, the country also faces significant challenges in these areas, including censorship and limited access to information. Addressing these challenges will require comprehensive policies and programs, as well as investment in technology and infrastructure. The ongoing promotion of free speech and press freedom is essential for building a more democratic and inclusive Nigerian society.

The Arts in Nigeria: Literature, Music, and Film

The arts have played a significant role in Nigerian culture, with literature, music, and film serving as important mediums for cultural expression and storytelling. Nigerian artists have gained international recognition for their work, contributing to a vibrant and diverse global cultural landscape. In this chapter, we will explore the rich cultural heritage of Nigerian arts and the contribution of artists to the global cultural scene.

Literature is one of the most significant forms of artistic expression in Nigeria, with a long tradition of storytelling and literary excellence. Nigerian writers have gained international recognition for their work, with authors such as Chinua Achebe, Wole Soyinka, and Chimamanda Ngozi Adichie becoming household names around the world. The Nigerian literary scene is diverse, with writers working in a variety of genres, including poetry, fiction, and drama.

Music is another significant form of artistic expression in Nigeria, with a rich history of traditional and contemporary musical styles. Nigerian music has gained international recognition, with artists such as Fela Kuti, King Sunny Ade, and Burna Boy becoming popular around the world. The Nigerian music scene is diverse, with artists working in a variety of genres, including Afrobeats, highlife, and juju music.

Film is also an important form of artistic expression in Nigeria, with a thriving film industry known as Nollywood. Nigerian films are known for their unique storytelling style and have gained international recognition, with Nollywood becoming the second-largest film industry in the world by volume. Nigerian films explore a variety of themes, including social issues, culture, and politics.

The arts in Nigeria face significant challenges, including inadequate funding and limited access to resources. However, there are also opportunities for promoting the arts and supporting the work of artists in Nigeria. The government has introduced various initiatives aimed at promoting the arts, including the establishment of the National Endowment for the Arts and the National Council for Arts and Culture.

The private sector has also played a significant role in promoting the arts in Nigeria, particularly through investment in music and film production. However, there is a need for greater collaboration between the public and private sectors to support the arts and ensure that artists have access to the resources they need to produce their work.

In conclusion, the arts have played a significant role in Nigerian culture, with literature, music, and film serving as important mediums for cultural expression and storytelling. Nigerian artists have gained international recognition for their work, contributing to a vibrant and diverse global cultural landscape. Addressing the challenges facing the arts in Nigeria will require comprehensive policies and programs, as well as investment in resources and infrastructure. The ongoing promotion of the arts is essential for building a more vibrant and inclusive Nigerian society.

Sports in Nigeria: Football, Athletics, and Other Popular Activities

Sports play a significant role in Nigerian culture, with football, athletics, and other activities serving as popular pastimes and sources of national pride. Nigerian athletes have gained international recognition, contributing to a vibrant and diverse global sports scene. In this chapter, we will explore the rich sporting heritage of Nigeria and the contribution of athletes to the global sports landscape.

Football is the most popular sport in Nigeria, with millions of Nigerians following the domestic and international football leagues. The Nigerian national football team, known as the Super Eagles, has achieved significant success on the international stage, winning the African Cup of Nations several times and competing in several World Cup tournaments. Nigerian footballers, including Nwankwo Kanu, Jay-Jay Okocha, and John Obi Mikel, have gained international recognition, playing for some of the world's most prominent football clubs.

Athletics is another significant sport in Nigeria, with a long tradition of excellence in track and field. Nigerian athletes have won several Olympic and World Championship medals in events such as sprinting, long jump, and triple jump. Nigerian athletes, including Chioma Ajunwa, Blessing Okagbare, and Ese Brume, have gained international recognition for their athletic achievements.

Other popular sports in Nigeria include basketball, boxing, and wrestling. Nigeria has a thriving basketball scene, with several Nigerian basketball players competing in the NBA, including Hakeem Olajuwon and Masai Ujiri. Nigerian boxers, including Dick Tiger and Samuel Peter, have also gained international recognition, competing at the highest levels of professional boxing.

The sports scene in Nigeria faces significant challenges, including inadequate funding and limited access to resources. However, there are also opportunities for promoting sports and supporting the work of athletes in Nigeria. The government has introduced various initiatives aimed at promoting sports, including the establishment of the National Sports Commission and the National Institute for Sports.

The private sector has also played a significant role in promoting sports in Nigeria, particularly through investment in football and basketball. However, there is a need for greater collaboration between the public and private sectors to support sports and ensure that athletes have access to the resources they need to compete at the highest levels.

In conclusion, sports play a significant role in Nigerian culture, with football, athletics, and other activities serving as popular pastimes and sources of national pride. Nigerian athletes have gained international recognition, contributing to a vibrant and diverse global sports scene. Addressing the challenges facing sports in Nigeria will require comprehensive policies and programs, as well as investment in resources and infrastructure. The ongoing promotion of sports is essential for building a more vibrant and inclusive Nigerian society.

Nigeria's Future: Challenges and Prospects for the 21st Century

Nigeria is a country with immense potential, but it also faces significant challenges as it moves into the 21st century. Addressing these challenges is essential for promoting economic growth, social development, and political stability in Nigeria. In this chapter, we will explore some of the challenges and prospects for Nigeria's future.

One of the significant challenges facing Nigeria is political instability. The country has experienced several periods of military rule and political turmoil, which have hindered its democratic development. Addressing these challenges will require comprehensive political reforms, including strengthening democratic institutions, promoting transparency and accountability, and improving governance.

Another significant challenge facing Nigeria is economic development. Despite its significant oil and gas reserves, Nigeria's economy remains heavily dependent on these resources, with limited diversification into other sectors. The country also faces significant challenges in infrastructure development, education, and healthcare. Addressing these challenges will require comprehensive economic reforms, including promoting economic diversification, investment in infrastructure and technology, and improving the quality of education and healthcare.

Nigeria also faces significant social challenges, including inequality, poverty, and social exclusion. The country has one of the highest rates of poverty in the world, with millions of Nigerians living in poverty. Addressing these challenges will require comprehensive social reforms, including promoting inclusive growth, improving access to education and healthcare, and reducing social exclusion.

Despite these challenges, there are also prospects for Nigeria's future. The country has a significant youth population, which could serve as a demographic dividend, contributing to economic growth and social development. Nigeria also has significant potential in renewable energy, agriculture, and manufacturing, which could help to diversify the economy and promote sustainable development.

Addressing the challenges and realizing the prospects for Nigeria's future will require comprehensive policies and programs, as well as investment in resources and infrastructure. The government must work to promote political stability, economic diversification, and social development, as well as address the challenges facing the country's environment and natural resources.

In conclusion, Nigeria is a country with immense potential, but it also faces significant challenges as it moves into the 21st century. Addressing these challenges is essential for promoting economic growth, social development, and political stability in Nigeria. The ongoing promotion of comprehensive policies and programs, as well as investment in resources and infrastructure, is essential for building a more vibrant, inclusive, and sustainable Nigerian society.

Conclusion

Nigeria is a country with a rich and diverse history, culture, and heritage. From the pre-colonial era to the present day, Nigeria has experienced significant social, economic, and political changes that have shaped its development and identity. This book has explored some of the key themes and events in Nigeria's history, highlighting the challenges and opportunities facing the country as it moves into the 21st century.

Throughout its history, Nigeria has faced significant challenges, including colonialism, military rule, political instability, economic inequality, and social exclusion. Despite these challenges, Nigeria has also experienced significant achievements, including independence, democratic transition, economic growth, and cultural diversity. Nigeria has also contributed significantly to the global cultural and sports scene, with artists and athletes gaining international recognition for their work.

The future of Nigeria will be shaped by how the country addresses the challenges and opportunities it faces. Addressing the challenges of political instability, economic development, and social inequality will require comprehensive policies and programs, as well as investment in resources and infrastructure. Building a more vibrant, inclusive, and sustainable Nigerian society will require promoting political stability, economic diversification, and social development, as well as addressing the challenges facing the country's environment and natural resources.

As Nigeria moves into the 21st century, it faces both significant challenges and prospects for the future. Nigeria has a significant youth population, a diverse cultural heritage, and a thriving arts and sports scene. These assets, along with strategic investment in infrastructure, education, and technology, can help to promote economic growth, social development, and political stability in Nigeria.

In conclusion, Nigeria's history is rich and diverse, with significant achievements and challenges. The country has contributed significantly to the global cultural and sports scene, and its future holds significant prospects for economic, social, and political development. Addressing the challenges facing the country will require comprehensive policies and programs, as well as investment in resources and infrastructure. Building a more vibrant, inclusive, and sustainable Nigerian society will require the ongoing promotion of political stability, economic diversification, and social development, as well as addressing the challenges facing the country's environment and natural resources. The future of Nigeria is in the hands of its people, and it is up to all Nigerians to work together to build a brighter future for the country.

Thank you for reading this book on Nigeria's history to modern times. We hope that it has provided you with a comprehensive understanding of the country's past, present, and future prospects. If you enjoyed the book and found it informative, we kindly ask you to leave a positive review. Your feedback is essential to us, and it helps us to improve our work and continue providing informative and engaging content to our readers. Thank you once again for your time and support.

Printed in Great Britain
by Amazon